GIRL TALK

How to survive

MEAN GIRLS

Lisa Miles and Xanna Eve Chown

rosen publishing's
rosen central

NEW YORK

This edition published in 2014 by:

The Rosen Publishing Group, Inc.
29 East 21st Street, New York, NY 10010

Copyright © 2014 Arcturus Publishing Limited

Designer: Jeni Child
Editor: Joe Harris
Consultants: Gill Lynas and Emma Hughes
Picture research: Lisa Miles and Xanna Eve Chown
With thanks to Bethany Miller
Picture credits: All images courtesy of Shutterstock

Library of Congress Cataloging-in-Publication Data

Miles, Lisa
How to survive mean girls/[Lisa Miles and Xanna Eve Chown].—1st ed.—New York: Rosen, c2014
        p. cm.—(Girl talk)
Includes index.
ISBN: 978-1-4777-0707-4 (Library Binding)
ISBN: 978-1-4777-0721-0 (Paperback)
ISBN: 978-1-4777-0722-7 (6-pack)
1. Teenage girls—psychology—Juvenile literature. 2. Female friendship—Juvenile literature. 3. Teenage girls—Juvenile Literature. 4. Interpersonal conflict in adolescence—Juvenile literature. I. Chown, Xanna Eve. II. Title.
HQ798 .M55 2014
305.23'5

Manufactured in China

CPSIA Compliance Information: Batch #S13YA: For further information, contact Rosen Publishing, New York, New York, at 1-800-237-9932.

Contents

and

being mean

Friends are really important to you, right? For almost everyone that's absolutely true. There's nothing like a friend to have fun with, share secrets with or to cheer you up when you feel down. But it doesn't always work out that way.

It's not always easy to make friends or to stay friends. Friendships sometimes hit a bump, just like other relationships. And in some circumstances, you might find yourself excluded from friendships—or even the victim of bullying from a group of girls who are intent on being mean to others. It's not nice, but it does happen.

Girl Talk is here to help you spot the difficulties that come with making friends, falling out with friends and facing mean girls who are definitely NOT your friends.

I think my best friend is really cool (but the matching hats have GOT to go!).

GIRL TO GIRL

"I've been friends with the girl who lives next door to me since we were six. When we started our new school, she began to hang out with girls whom I found hard to get along with. At first I was really sad, but then I realized that I could make new friends, too. Ella is still my friend but I don't think she's my best friend anymore."

"I fell out with my friend big time. We had a huge fight over something silly and she made me cry. The next day she came by, she said sorry and gave me a huge hug. I was so relieved. I didn't want to lose my best friend over something that didn't really matter all that much to either of us."

"Some girls that I don't even know ganged up on me. They teased me about the clothes I was wearing and then they started calling me names. It went on for a week and I was starting to feel scared, but then they suddenly dropped me. I think they started picking on someone else."

Friends... and falling out

Stories from my life

I've been best friends with Sophie forever and we used to hang out together all the time. But, recently, things have changed...

Sophie joined the film club and she's made some new friends – Kyla and Lucy. I'm not jealous; I just don't think I like them. Whenever she's chatting with them, I can see they're laughing and then looking over at some of the other girls in our class. It's pretty obvious that they're not saying anything nice.

I tried going over and joining in, but they kind of shut up and acted like there was some big joke, and I wasn't in on it. I told Kyla I liked her necklace – it had a silver "K" on it. She told me I should get one with an "L" on it – for loser. Then she laughed and said she was just kidding. Sophie laughed too, but I felt really bad.

I can't help thinking... maybe I'm the joke?

Am I really a loser?

THE LOWDOWN

Real-life advice

If girls you think are your friends keep picking on you, they're not really your friends. You can find someone else to hang out with. Have fun with other people and don't let the mean girls stop you!

Why do girls form cliques?

A clique is a group of friends who all like to act – and probably dress – the same way. Not everyone who would like to join their group is allowed to. In fact, the members of the clique probably love the fact that they are an exclusive group. It makes them feel popular and cool. Girls in a clique do everything together – and sometimes that includes bullying. Putting other people down is an easy way to feel better about themselves.

ARE YOU BEING left out?

Being the outsider

When you're part of a friendship group, it's great to feel included and share all the gossip and in-jokes with your friends. But it's not so great if you suddenly find yourself on the outside looking in.

Feeling left out can be really painful, especially if you don't really understand why it's happening. It could be that your friends don't know they're leaving you out. Maybe they arranged to go somewhere together and genuinely forgot to ask you. Or perhaps they are sharing a joke that they think you won't find funny.

I wonder what they're laughing about?

TOP FIVE... worst things about being in a clique

1 Feeling peer pressure.

2 Having to hang out with the whole group all the time, instead of just being with your best friend sometimes.

3 Worrying about being dropped from the group.

4 Being dropped from the group – and being sad about it.

5 Knowing outsiders are definitely not welcome.

If you constantly feel like you're being pushed out of a friendship group, ask one of the group if you can speak to her alone and tell her. Your friends may not realize they're being mean. But if it seems like they don't really care about how you feel, maybe it's time to look elsewhere for friendship.

GIRL TALK

Real-life advice

If you're feeling left out, try organizing a day out or at your house for the whole group to show your friends you want to hang out with them.

FEELING different?

People change as they grow up because they find new interests or go through new experiences. This means that friends can sometimes grow apart, even though they still care about each other.

Not fitting in?

Perhaps the friends you've grown up with are no longer your style. You might have different things you want to do, or a different fashion sense. Or maybe you just don't understand each other any more. It's normal to drift apart, but it can be difficult to make the break without being mean.

The best thing is to keep your options open. Mix with different girls in your class, join a club or sit with a different group at lunchtime. You don't have to cut yourself off from your old friends overnight, but it may do you all good to have a change.

I remember when this bench used to be a lot more fun.

All about you   The friendship factor

Everyone looks for slightly different things in a friend, but there are some qualities that ALL good friends have in common: you should be able to trust them; they should care about you; and they should stick with you even if you're down.

If you're feeling confused about the friendship group you're in or about one particular friend, jot down the qualities YOU look for in a friend. It might help you decide where to go from here.

My friend should like sparkly lights, cats, nail polish and... er... me?

WHAT I LOOK FOR
IN A FRIEND:

Honest

Caring

Fun

Sensible?

Into music?

GiRL TALK

Real-life advice

You should never try to change what you like to fit in with other people. Being different is good. Real friends will accept that – and so should you!

FINDING friends

I f you have fallen out with your friends, don't despair. You have two options – you can either make up with them, or you can go out and find new friends. The second option may sound scary, but there are things you can do to make friends more easily.

Smile

Making friends is easier if you feel confident about yourself. Approaching new people with a smile and a friendly hello helps to break the ice. Engaging someone in small talk – such as chatting about what's for lunch – can lead to more conversation and gradually getting to know someone better. Take an interest in the other girls around you – ask them how they are or how they found the homework this week. You'll soon find that they'll be talking back to you in the same way.

Small talk means chatting about any little thing – even math!

Another way to meet new people is to join a club or take up a new activity, because it's easier making friends with people who have the same interests as you. So if there's something you've always wanted to try, then pluck up the courage and do it! You might find lots of new friends just waiting around the corner.

TALKING *Point*

Have you ever had to go out and make friends in a new situation? How did it feel?

GIRL TO GIRL

"I joined a new school mid-year and didn't know anyone. I felt really nervous and didn't dare to speak. Then a girl in my class asked me to sit with her at lunch and suddenly I felt normal again. It was great to have people to talk to."

"I fell out with my best friends because they wanted to go to places that I didn't. I was determined not to get down about it, so I asked another girl I know if she wanted to go to the movies with me. And she said yes!"

"I always wanted to try karate, and my friends thought I was crazy. But I went along to a karate class and loved it. The other people in the class were really fun and now I've got loads of new friends as well as my old ones. They still think I'm crazy, but that's okay!"

HOW TO BE A GOOD
friend!

Making friends can often come naturally, and you'll probably find that you fall in with girls you get along really well with. Friends are important – so remember to look after them!

Be nice – not nasty!

Being friends with someone means being kind to each other – and having a lot of fun! But try to remember these golden rules, too:

* **Do listen to her.** Find out what she likes and what's important to her.

* **Do be sensitive to her feelings.** Remember things that might upset her.

* **Do help her with her problems.** Everyone needs help sometimes.

* **Don't tease her or mock her.** Even if you think it's funny, she probably won't.

* **Don't gossip about her behind her back.** That's just mean.

TOP FIVE... best things about having a best friend!

1. *You have the MOST fun when you're with her.*

2. *She knows your secrets – even the embarrassing ones!*

3. *She doesn't mind (much) if you talk about your crush all the time!*

4. *She knows what you're thinking – without having to ask you!*

5. *She's there when you need a hug.*

THE LOWDOWN

Saying sorry

Being a good friend also means knowing when to say sorry. So if you've been a bit mean or if you accidentally said or did the wrong thing, then it's best to show you care and apologize. It's not always easy to say sorry, but if your friend means a lot to you, then it's worth the effort and she will appreciate your saying it.

WHAT SORT OF FRIEND
are you?

Do you keep falling out with your friend? Should you try harder to be a good friend to her? Answer the questions and follow the arrows to find out!

START HERE!

You argue about little things – like who has the best taste in music!

NO

YES

You like the same boys at the same time!

YES

NO

You are always interested in what other people think.

YES

NO

You argue about more important stuff – like boys!

YES

NO

When you fight, you always make up again quickly!

NO

YES

Once you've made your mind up about something, that's it!

YES

NO

COULD DO BETTER!

Remember that friendships need some give and take! If you're not careful, you might lose your friend.

You always say sorry when you are in the wrong.

NO

YES

You always think fights are her fault – not yours.

NO

YES

A GOOD FRIEND

Is something bugging you about your friendship? Talk things through, and you'll get back on track.

You always like to talk things through to work out what went wrong.

NO

YES

A GREAT FRIEND

You're great at making up and your fights are only small ones. It sounds like your friendship is for keeps!

Other friends have to help you sort out arguments.

YES

NO

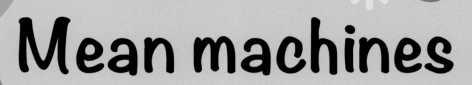

Mean machines

Stories from my life

I decided the best thing to do was to avoid Sophie and her new friends. So, all week at school I've been hanging with some of my other friends – and feeling totally miserable! I mean, they're all right, but they're just not Sophie.

Then Sophie phoned me up after school today, sounding really sad. She asked me why I was avoiding her! We ended up having a massive heart-to-heart. I said sorry for avoiding her. Then I told her how bad her friends were making me feel and SHE told me they made her feel bad too! She didn't like the way they said mean things all the time.

We're going to hang out again, and I'm so happy. But I'm a bit worried for Sophie – I don't think Kyla will be happy to let Sophie go just like that...

We're friends again - hurray!

Keeping it real:
Had a fight with a friend? Deal with it!

☑ **Calm down.** If you have had a fight with a friend, give it some time before trying to sort it out.

☑ **Say sorry.** Chances are you have both done something wrong. You will gain respect by being mature and apologizing.

☑ **Don't get defensive.** The best thing to do with criticism is learn from it. Try to understand where your friend is coming from.

☑ **Stand up for yourself.** Don't let anyone walk over you. If you have a point to make, you should make it.

☑ **Agree to disagree.** It's fine to have a difference of opinion on some subjects. It shouldn't get in the way of a friendship.

TALKING Point

Have YOU ever had a fight with a friend? How did you both get over it?

Bullying – WHAT IS IT?

If you are being bullied you could be intimidated, threatened, physically abused, called names or made to feel small. Bullies can be people you think are your friends.

Bullying can make you feel scared or upset. It can affect your schoolwork, your self-esteem, and the way you behave at home.

✳ **Physical bullying can include:**

Hitting
Banging
Tripping
Punching
Shoving

✳ **Verbal bullying can include:**

Malicious gossip
Name-calling
Taunting
Teasing
Excluding people

Studies show that boys are more likely to be physical bullies, and girls verbal, but it's not always that way. Girls can hit, and boys can spread rumors, too.

20

THE LOWDOWN

Why do people get bullied?

Say NO to bullying!

Some people seem to be bullied more than others. This is because bullies often pick on certain people: those they are jealous of; those they think will not fight back; and those they think don't fit in. People get bullied because of looks, race, religion, how much money they have, the clothes they wear or the way they act. But these are not reasons – they are excuses. Bullying is always wrong.

BULLYING

GIRL TALK

Real-life advice

If you don't feel you can talk to a friend or family member, there are plenty of Web sites and helplines offering advice on how to beat bullying. Sometimes it's easier to talk to a stranger at first.

Surviving
CYBERBULLYING

Cyberbullying is the use of technology to bully someone. This can include texts, e-mails, tweets, posts, messages and online threats. It could involve posting personal information about a person without their consent or creating videos to hurt or embarrass them.

Cyberbullies can't cause physical pain, but they can have a huge effect on the way we live our lives, and they can be hard to avoid.

Someone's changed my status to say I love Justin Bieber! Noooo!

Keeping it real:
How to stay safe online

☑ **Stay away from Web sites used by bullies.** Block e-mail addresses and mobile numbers that send nasty messages.

☑ **Protect your password.** Keep your information safe.

☑ **Never give out your personal details.** That includes your mobile number, e-mail and address.

☑ **Check friends' lists on social networking sites.** Make sure you are only connected to people you know and like.

☑ **Find out where the "report abuse" and "block sender" options are on Web sites.** Use them if you need to.

☑ **Keep evidence of bullying.** Take screenshots, make a note of bullies' names and don't delete texts or e-mails.

☑ **Most importantly**, always tell an adult what is happening.

TALKING Point

What is your online experience? Have you ever posted anything online that you regret? Or has anyone ever put up a picture of you that you really hate?

MAKE A *change*

You'll never believe this!

Many girls are bullies, both in school and outside school. Some people become bullies because they have been bullied in the past. Sometimes they bully to feel part of a group. Some people don't even realize they are bullies.

Are you a bully?

Try to think about what effect your behavior has on the person you are bullying. How would you feel if it were you? Why do you behave like this? Does it really make you feel good about yourself?

Spreading rumors can be a form of bullying.

Are you friends with a bully?

If your friends bully others, try to talk to them about what they are doing. You don't need to join in, and you shouldn't just ignore it. It's your responsibility to tell an adult and encourage the bullied person to speak up, too.

THE LOWDOWN

What if an adult is bullying you?

If you feel that you are being unfairly singled out and treated with contempt by an adult, such as a teacher, you need to tell your parents or another adult. If you make accusations about an adult, there could be serious consequences for them – so be sure you are quite certain of your facts.

It can be hard to speak up, but you CAN make a difference.

DEALING WITH bullies

If you are being bullied, well-meaning people may tell you to try to ignore it, or that bullies are just cowards. However, you may need a better action plan.

Talk to friends. Don't keep bullying a secret.

Give this a try

If you ever get picked on by someone, here are some ideas to try:

* Avoid the bully and try to stick near friends. Make sure you are always with someone on the bus, in class and at break times.

* Practice not reacting to the bully's mean words. This is hard, but if you manage not to cry or get angry, you may be depriving the bully of the reaction he or she wants.

* Work out what it is the bully is doing that you want to stop. Then see if you can find the courage to talk to the bully about it. For example: "Please stop sending mean texts about me to everyone in the class." Then walk away.

* When you walk away, make sure you head to a safe area – a room with a teacher in it, or a group of adults you see in the street or park.

* Never threaten to hurt the bully. This is likely to lead to more bullying.

Keeping it real:
Talk to your parents

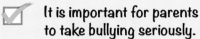

☑ **It is important for parents to take bullying seriously.** They should listen and not brush it off as something that is a natural part of childhood. Sit down with your parents at a quiet moment, tell them what's happening and how you are feeling.

☑ **Ask for their help.** Talk about what you can all do about the problem together. There might be ways they can help you be more assertive so that you can face the bullies more confidently.

☑ **Decide together.** Who might be the best person to help sort it out? Your parents might not want to talk to the bully's parents directly, so perhaps a teacher or counselor at the school will mediate.

THE LOWDOWN

Hazing – what's that?

Hazing is when a group, such as a club or sports team, demands that anyone who wants to join must perform dares. Sometimes these are just silly pranks, but sometimes they are harmful. Remember – you don't have to do anything that makes you feel uncomfortable. No one has a right to hurt you.

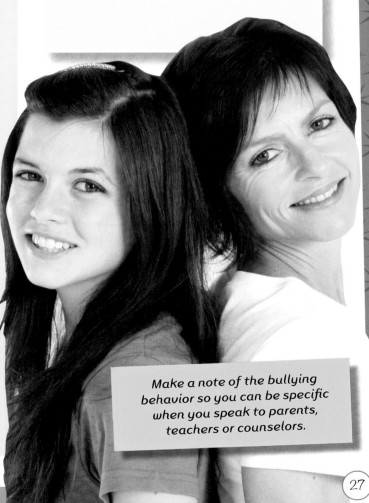

Make a note of the bullying behavior so you can be specific when you speak to parents, teachers or counselors.

ARE YOU A
mean girl?

nswer the questions (honestly!) then count up the number of As, Bs and Cs you have written down. Then check your score!

1 Do you make mean faces at others?
a *Yes, often*
b *Yes, sometimes*
c *No, never*

2 Do you say mean things behind people's backs?
a *Yes, often*
b *Yes, sometimes*
c *No, never*

3 Do you ever make people do things they don't want to do?
a *Yes, often*
b *Yes, sometimes*
c *No, never*

4 Do you ever call people rude names to their face?
a *Yes, often*
b *Yes, sometimes*
c *No, never*

Many dropouts mention bullying as the main reason they left school.

5 Do you ever hit other people?
a *Yes, often*
b *Yes, sometimes*
c *No, never*

6 Do you make fun of people because of the way they look?
a *Yes, often*
b *Yes, sometimes*
c *No, never*

7 Do you ever tell people that they can't hang out with you?
a *Yes, often*
b *Yes, sometimes*
c *No, never*

8 Do you tease people?
a *Yes, often*
b *Yes, sometimes*
c *No, never*

9 Do you whisper secrets in front of others and not share the secret?
a *Yes, often*
b *Yes, sometimes*
c *No, never*

10 Do you make fun of people for being shy?
a *Yes, often*
b *Yes, sometimes*
c *No, never*

Mostly As

Are you aware you are involved in bullying behavior? Sometimes we join in without thinking about how other people might be feeling. You need to think about what's been happening and change your behavior now.

Mostly Bs

You may have got involved in behavior that targeted other people. Perhaps you thought it was funny, or maybe you just watched and did nothing to help. Ask yourself what sort of person you would REALLY like to be – and act on it.

Mostly Cs

You're not a bully and that's great! It can take a lot of courage and confidence to stand up to others and not join in with any behavior that makes you uncomfortable. If you see other people being bullied, you should NEVER stand and watch.

Peer pressure – and how to beat it

Stories from my life

So, Kyla came over at lunch – acting super-friendly to Sophie and TOTALLY ignoring me. She asked Sophie if she wanted to watch the boys play football. I asked if I could come, but Kyla laughed and said she thought I was too young to be interested in boys!

I said: "If you haven't got anything nice to say, don't say anything." I'd been practicing saying it, so I didn't sound scared (and I think it worked!).

Sophie said she'd rather stay with me. Kyla told her she should be more picky about who she hangs out with! Sophie said she'd rather have a friend who wasn't mean all the time, and guess what? Kyla shrugged and walked away! It's great to have Sophie back.

It's SO good to be friends with Sophie again!

GIRL TO GIRL

"I hated school and didn't have any friends. Then I got a weekend job. If you are worried about friends, get a job or try a new activity. Doing something different helps you make new friends from all walks of life."

"When I got picked on at school, I tried to have some answers ready, like 'Calling me a coward won't make you brave,' or 'You can't judge me if you don't know me.' I wouldn't stay and fight, but just say one of my answers, and then walk away and tell a teacher what happened."

"If girls are being mean about you, the best thing to do is not to let it get to you. You shouldn't let them get in the way of your life and your schoolwork. Once I went up to a girl who was spreading rumors and confronted her – but with a smile and a friendly voice. I think she was so confused by that, she stopped."

PEER pressure
– WHAT'S THAT?

When you're hanging around with a group of friends, you want to fit in with them, right? And to fit in, you obviously want to do what they're doing – or do you?

Don't get pushed

Peer pressure is a term for when someone is persuaded to do something because they don't want to be left out. Peer pressure can be good – for instance, if everyone is doing well at school it can push you to do better, too. But peer pressure can be a bad thing if your friends encourage you to participate in risky behavior that, deep down, you don't want to get involved in. Don't get pushed into doing something that you really don't want to, even if everyone else is.

Give us your pocket money – everybody else is!

Keeping it real:
Know the risks

Are you being asked to do something that you're not sure about? Know the consequences before you decide. These are some of the risks:

☑ **Alcohol.** Embarrassing behavior, bad decision-making, and addiction (which can lead to diseases, mood swings and thinking problems).

☑ **Bullying.** Hurting someone else and damaging your own reputation as a good person.

☑ **Recreational drugs.** Danger of unknowingly taking toxic substances, changes in your thinking and behavior, failing at school, ill health and addiction.

☑ **Sex.** Pregnancy and sexually transmitted diseases.

☑ **Smoking.** Addiction, bad breath, breathing difficulties, developing diseases and exposing your family to passive smoking.

Don't forget, there are legal age limits attached to purchasing alcohol, tobacco and having sex. And recreational drugs are illegal.

You know you DON'T want to!

TALKING Point

Have you ever been asked to do something you didn't want to do? Did you say yes or no?

IT'S OK TO
say no!

Stand up for yourself!

It's often hard to say no, even when you want to. But if you feel uncomfortable about doing something, then it IS perfectly OK to say no. You just have to learn how to do it.

The best way to avoid being pressured into doing something is to have confidence in yourself. Self-esteem is very important in helping you to stand up for what you think is right. If you stay strong and behave in a way that is right for you, then you're also setting a good example for your friends!

So if your friends try to pressure you into something you're not sure about, just say no. You don't have to make a fuss or give a big explanation. Say, "No, I'm not really into that," and take yourself away from the situation. If you get a hard time from your friends because of it, the chances are, they're not really your friends.

Saying no is easy once you've got the knack!

All about you — Practice makes perfect!

A good way to practice saying no is to say it in situations where it doesn't really matter. For instance, if you get approached in the street by a salesperson, say no politely and firmly, without hesitating, and walk on. You can also practice saying no in front of the mirror at home. Stand tall, smile and say, "No, I don't want to," or "No, I'd rather not." See, it's easy!

No? No. No! No...

Friends. Just because they're cool doesn't mean they are always right!

FEELING lonely?

If you've been the victim of bullying or peer pressure and you've lost friends because of it, you're probably feeling rejected and maybe even totally friendless. Try not to worry if you feel lonely. Things can change.

Beating the blues!

If you feel friendless, it's important not to get bitter and give up on people in general. Just because you were treated meanly by one set of friends, it doesn't mean that everyone is like that. It's tempting to shut yourself away to protect yourself from being hurt again, but that's not going to help in the long run.

Instead, make sure you get out of the house regularly – and not just to school!

If you think someone is feeling lonely, remember to be a good friend. Check on how she is doing and include her from time to time.

From other people's point of view, it's not always that easy to spot loneliness. Someone who seems happy and busy on the outside can be feeling lonely and sad on the inside. So if you feel lonely, tell someone how you feel – if you confide in someone, they'll probably be glad to help. And remember that you, too, have to be friendly to get friends.

Keeping it real:
Making new friends

Here are some tips to help you reconnect with life – and friends!

☑ **Call an old friend.** Invite her to do something with you, such as go to the movies or go for a bike ride.

☑ **Join a new group or club.** It's a great way to meet new people.

☑ **Take a walk in the park.** It will help you feel like you're part of the world and not alone.

☑ **Aim to be a rounded person.** Have more than one set of interests, and you'll soon feel more connected.

THE LOWDOWN

Three's a crowd?

It's easy to feel lonely sometimes, even when you ARE part of a group. This often happens when girls team up in a threesome. There's always the risk that two of the three will bond more closely and the third will feel left out. There's not much you can do about this except try not to mind, stay friends but also look outside the group for other friendships. At the end of the day, you have to accept other people's friendships – as they have to accept yours.

DO YOU KNOW THE FACTS ABOUT bullying?

Some people see bullying as a fact of life, but it doesn't have to be that way. Today, more adults are trained to help put an end to bullying, especially in schools. They know the facts. Try these questions and see if you do, too.

1. When does bullying mostly take place?
A – After school
B – During lessons
C – At break times

2. A victim of bullying is most likely to be...
A – Older than the bully
B – Younger than the bully
C – The same age as the bully

3. What is the most common reaction to bullying?
A – To tell a teacher
B – To keep it to themselves
C – To tell their parents

4. In what situation does most bullying happen?
A – When there are no adults watching
B – When there are adults watching
C – When there are no other kids watching

5. What is a common characteristic of bullies?

A – *High level of social skills*
B – *Low level of social skills*
C – *Medium level of social skills*

6. Students who are bullied are more likely to...

A – *Stay in school*
B – *Leave school early*
C – *Get really good jobs*

HOW MANY DID YOU GET RIGHT?

1-3	4-6	7-10
Uh-oh!	Not bad!	Good job!

7. What do most students say they do if they witness bullying?

A – *They try to help*
B – *Nothing, but they feel bad about it*
C – *Nothing, because it's not their problem*

8. Is it possible for bullies to change their ways?

A – *No, once a bully, always a bully*
B – *Yes, if something happens to stop them*
C – *Yes, they will stop bullying if they are ignored*

THE LOWDOWN

If you got some questions wrong, make sure you look at what the correct answer was – and make sure you understand why it was the right one. If you don't know, talk it through with a friend or an adult. It's good to be in the know when it comes to bullying.

ANSWERS

1. C	5. A
2. B	6. B
3. B	7. C
4. A	8. B

Boy talk

FROM HIS POINT OF VIEW

Boys are more likely than girls to be physical bullies, which means that they push, punch, kick or yell at other boys. Adults may dismiss this as a "natural" part of male childhood – but they shouldn't.

Who's in charge? Let's find out... with our fists!

All about power

Boys who bully want to show how powerful they are. They often target boys who are quiet and don't have many friends. They can create problems in the classroom with disruptive behavior and act as if they are proud of what they have done – because their actions match what they believe to be "masculine" behavior.

Boys do bully girls as well as other boys. This can include name calling, spreading gossip or trying to force them into doing things they don't want to do. This can have serious consequences and should always be reported.

BOYS SAY...

"I've heard that boys bully according to what group they are in. So the ones that like sports might bully the ones that don't. But girls bully people according to whether they are popular or not."

"Boys get bullied by girls too. I had some upper-lip hair that was dark and these two girls picked on me for it. They kept shouting, 'You've got a moustache!' until I was really upset. I didn't want to tell anyone, because it was girls that did it."

"My friend told me some stupid stories about his girlfriend. He thought it was funny, but I think it's unfair. His girlfriend didn't know he was saying those things about her. I think he should have showed her a bit more respect."

HEALTHY you!

In order to be in good shape, you need to be healthy AND happy! Your mental health and emotional state can be just as important as your physical well-being.

Low self-esteem – why it's a health problem

If you have low self-esteem, it means that you don't value yourself properly as a person. You might criticize yourself too much, you might often be unhappy or you might be the victim of bullying. Low self-esteem is serious because it can cause mental and emotional health problems, such as stress, anxiety and depression.

If that sounds like you, then it's wise to get some help. Talk to your parents or to someone who can offer professional advice, such as a teacher, a health worker or school counselor. Don't let low self-esteem dominate YOUR life.

Don't lock in your feelings – tell someone who can help you.

Keeping it real:

Girl power!

There are lots of things you can do to boost your confidence and improve your self-esteem. Try these!

☑ **Make a list!** Write down all the things you're good at. It can be anything from baking cookies or taking photos to something sporty.

☑ **Write a "positive" diary.** Write down good things that happen to you or positive thoughts you have during the day. When you feel down, you can look back and give yourself a boost.

☑ **Find a role model.** Pick a hero who is talented in some way, gives something back to society and cares about who they are – and not necessarily what they look like.

☑ **Have an ambition.** Think of something you really want to do, such as go on a special trip or get an amazing job, and make a plan for how you're going to do that one day.

☑ **Create your own style.** Don't feel pushed into following the latest fashions if you don't like them or they're not right for you. Look good in your own way.

☑ **Excel at something!** Find a skill or activity that you're good at – even if your friends aren't interested in the same thing. Let yourself flourish – and maybe make new friends, too.

FAQs

Q **A** My friend is being picked on at school but she won't tell. I don't understand why not.

There could be several reasons. Often young people are taught not to tell tales. It might be that they have told someone what is happening before, but nothing has been done about it, or they haven't been believed. They may feel embarrassed about what is going on and not want to admit to it, or feel ashamed that they can't deal with the situation alone. Some people may not want to worry their parents, so they keep things to themselves. Encourage your friend to tell someone – or perhaps you could do it for her if she agrees?

Spreading – or even listening to – malicious gossip is a form of bullying.

Q **A** My friend has turned into a mean girl! How do girls get mean?

Psychologist Charisse Nixon believes that girls have a few basic needs. She calls these "ABCs and ME," which stands for Acceptance, Belonging, Control and Meaningful Existence. When those needs aren't met, girls sometimes do mean things to meet them. Mean girls use teasing and gossip and other types of bullying to improve their social position. Their need to be at the top of the popularity charts may reflect a lack of control they feel in other areas of their life.

 My mom says my friend is toxic. What does that mean?

 A toxic friend may act like she is your friend, and even think she is your friend – but you might feel it's more complicated. Friends should be supportive, but a toxic friend may say hurtful things – and tell you it is for your own good. A toxic friend may try to stop you from having other friends, or always want to tell you what to do. No friend should make you feel uncomfortable or put you down.

 I'm being picked on by a girl at school. Why me?

Sometimes a mean girl's focus is someone who stands out from the crowd, perhaps because of her appearance or the way she acts. Sometimes the girl being picked on has said the "wrong" thing – talking to someone's boyfriend or being too friendly with a teacher. Cruelty can often be motivated by jealousy.

 How can I stop being bullied?

Don't try to handle the problem by yourself. Tell a friend, your parents or a school guidance counselor and let them help. Never ignore the problem or try to get revenge as these tactics can backfire. If you can stand up for yourself and show bullies you're not intimidated, they may stop. If you see someone being picked on, don't feel grateful it's not you and join in. That's not cool.

Glossary

addiction A compulsive need for a substance that is known by the user to be harmful.

ambition A strong desire to achieve success in a particular area.

assertive Confident or bold in behavior and speech.

clique A small group of people who spend time together and exclude others.

confide To tell someone something that is secret or private, and to expect them not to tell anyone else.

contempt A lack of respect.

cyberbullying Using technology to bully other people, for example, with text messages and e-mails or via Web sites and social forums.

depression A state of mind or mental disorder often marked by feelings of hopelessness and dejection.

excel To stand out due to being especially good at something.

exclude To leave out deliberately.

intimidate To frighten someone with threats or by force of personality, especially to make the person do what you want.

jealous Feeling envious of someone else and their achievements, or feeling suspicious that one's partner is being unfaithful.

mediate To attempt to settle differences or problems by working with everyone involved to come to an agreement.

outsider A person who does not belong to a particular group.

peer pressure Strong influence from members of one's peer group (people one's own age, such as classmates).

recreational drugs Drugs that are used for personal enjoyment rather than for a medical reason.

self-esteem A sense of of pride and respect for oneself.

taunt To provoke someone with insulting or unkind remarks.

toxic Extremely malicious or harmful; poisonous.

Get help!

There are places to go to if you need more help. The following books and Web sites will give you more information and advice.

Further reading

Cyberbullying (True Books: Guides to Life) by Lucy Raatma (Scholastic, 2013)

Girls Against Girls: Why We Are Mean to Each Other and How We Can Change by Bonnie Burton (Zest Books, 2009)

How to Win Friends and Influence People for Girls by Donna Dale Carnegie (Vermilion, 2006)

Mean Chicks, Cliques, and Dirty Tricks: A Real Girl's Guide to Getting Through It All by Erika V. Shearin Karres (Adams Media, 2010)

Stand Up for Yourself and Your Friends: Dealing with Bullies and Bossiness, and Finding a Better Way by Patti Kelley Criswell (American Girl Publishing, Inc., 2008)

Top 10 Tips for Building Friendships (Tips for Success) by Dale-Marie Bryan (Rosen Publishing, 2013)

Web sites

Due to the changing nature of Internet links, Rosen Publishing has developed an online list of Web sites related to the subject of this book. This site is updated regularly. Please use this link to access the list:

http://www.rosenlinks.com/GTALK/Mean

Index